MENTAL ILLNESS AND YOUR MARRIAGE

PRAISE FOR THIS BOOK

This book is a practical and powerful guide to helping couples cope with mental illness when it invades a marriage. Jim and Leah speak personally and practically about the tasks necessary to keep the marriage functional and on the path to healing.

—Rev. Dr. Raymond Pendleton
Senior Professor of Counseling
Gordon-Conwell Theological Seminary

Rev. Dr. Jim Stout and Rev. Leah Stout write honestly about the impact of Jim's bipolar illness on their marriage. The book goes beyond to sharing actionable ways to jumpstart a floundering marriage. Anyone in a marriage where one of the spouses has a mental illness ought to read this book.

—Karen Mason, Ph.D., L.P.C.
Professor of Counseling and Psychology
Director of the Hamilton Counseling Program
Gordon-Conwell Theological Seminary

Jim Stout's books directly provide concrete lessons that teach and inspire both those who are mentally well and mentally ill. Even when we are down, we retain our unique character and inviolability as men and women of God! I have been personally mentored by Jim Stout and find his works and our unique relationship are grounded in God's persistence and our perseverance. Jim's books provide straightforward tools that lead to inspiration and results for both those afflicted with a mental illness and their loved ones.

—Ken Stokes

Rev. Stout offers a realistic and yet hopeful work-in-progress that is called marriage. His background in dealing with mental health issues in his own marriage make this book a contribution for so many who could lose hope quickly in a marriage without a door to true recovery. A necessary resource for couples and those who work in the field of relationships.

—Rev. Cliff Ishigaki
Trauma recovery specialist

ALSO BY JIM STOUT

MENTAL ILLNESS AND YOUR MARRIAGE

JIM STOUT

LEAH STOUT

SHEPHERD PUBLISHING

The information in this book is intended to complement, not substitute for, the advice of your physician, psychiatrist, psychologist, MFT, MSW, or other mental-medical health provider. Please consult him or her about your unique needs. If you are in urgent difficulty, phone 911 or a crisis hotline, such as the National Suicide Prevention Crisis Hotline at 1-800-273-TALK (1-800-273-8255).

Edited by Andrew Kroeger and Stephanie Starr

Proofread by Elijah Dove

Designed and Produced by Barton Hill Books at bartonhillbooks.com

Printed in the United States of America

Published by Shepherd Publishing

Visit www.drjimstout.com

ISBN: 978-1-942648-14-7

CONTENTS

DEDICATED WITH GRATITUDE

To our therapists, Phil Sutherland, David Stoop, Dae Leckie, Keith Edwards, and Michelle McCormick, who gave patient support and guidance.

To our friends, who supported both of us with patient listening and unconditional love.

To our Great Counselor, Jesus Christ, who comforted and guided us through our long maze of relationship issues.

AUTHOR'S NOTE

For the reader's convenience, and for clarification, we have used either *he* or *she* rather than the longer *he and/or she* for brevity when referring to men or women. In most cases, *he* or *she* is intended to refer to anyone, regardless of gender.

INTRODUCTION

Beginning in the fall of 1988, Jim was voluntarily hospitalized in two psychiatric facilities. Finally, after nearly six months, he was discharged with a diagnosis of bipolar disorder.

Jim's bipolar diagnosis changed a lot of things for us, and since then we've learned many things about ourselves and our relationship. His hospitalization and diagnosis presented us with two major challenges: first, it forced us to deal with some longstanding issues in our relationship, and second, the complications of his mental disorder introduced us to a whole new way to live.

Mental Illness and Your Marriage is an expanded version of a keynote address we gave at the 2002 NAMI (National Alliance on Mental Illness) California Conference. Our presentation was ruthlessly honest, yet infused with hope and practical help.

The positive responses from spouses living with mentally ill partners was overwhelming. But the thing that surprised both the conference leaders and us was the enthusiastic response from couples who *weren't* struggling with the effects of mental illness. So, whether your marriage involves mental "problems" or just faces "normal" marital struggles, we hope you will find this book helpful.

Saving and rehabilitating our marriage has been a long, painful process, but it's been well worth the time, effort, money, and emotional turmoil. We've learned, and are still learning, valuable lessons in healing and enhancing our relationship. While we earnestly desire to be a blessing to each other, we also want to be a blessing to other couples.

The purpose of *Mental Illness and Your Marriage* is to share our experiences and offer practical tips and strategies for you to implement in your marriage. We share our knowledge with the hope that other marriages might be healed, strengthened, and spared the pain of divorce.

Our approach is similar to D. T. Niles's description of evangelism: "One beggar sharing with another beggar where to find bread."

As in our original NAMI keynote talk, the chapters ahead are arranged as an interview. We will begin by providing some information about mental illness and marriage, and will then share our personal stories. Next, both of us will answer the same three questions from our own perspectives:

1. How has bipolar disorder affected your marriage?
2. How have you coped with the effects of bipolar disorder?
3. What have you done to heal your marriage?

We then share some actionable ways to jumpstart your marriage healing process, and conclude with a chapter about what to do if a spouse is unwilling to get help for his or her mental illness.

As you read our words, please apply a slogan from Alcoholics Anonymous: "Take what works and leave the rest."

1

WHY TALK ABOUT MENTAL ILLNESS AND MARRIAGE?

Marriage is like life in this—that it is a field of battle, not a bed of roses.
Robert Louis Stevenson

While divorce statistics vary somewhat from study to study and year to year, their numbers aren't too far apart. In the US and Canada, at least 40 percent of *all* marriages fail.[1] Divorce statistics for marriages where one person has bipolar disorder are worse—it is estimated that *90 percent* end in divorce![2]

The "bible" for mental health providers is the *Diagnostic and Statistical Manual of Mental Disorders,* commonly known as *DSM-5™.* It lists more than 300 mental disorders. Some of the more common ones are: clinical depression, schizophrenia, bipolar disorder, dementia, and anxiety. Each of these disorders bring changes in thinking, mood, personality, personal habits, or social withdrawal.

Symptoms of a mental illness may include mild to

severe disturbances in thoughts or behaviors (or both) which result in an inability to cope with life's ordinary demands and routines.

Even though every disorder has a unique set of symptoms, characteristics, and specialized treatments, mental disorders generally have many traits in common and can lead to similar marital problems.

In the case of bipolar disorder, multiple studies show that without effective treatment (at minimum: medication and counseling) it is rare for a bipolar person to become healthy or stay healthy. In fact, without treatment, bipolar disorder (as with many other mental illnesses) almost always *worsens*.

For untreated bipolar sufferers in *depressive* periods, there can be an increase in harmful depressive symptoms such as:

- irritability;
- emotional numbness;
- sleep difficulties;
- anxiety;
- problems with physical health;
- overwhelming emotional pain;
- procrastination;
- withdrawal from people;
- avoidance of phone calls;
- lack of motivation;
- inability to concentrate;
- poor memory;
- inability to experience pleasure;
- sense of failure;
- extreme guilt;

- self-condemnation;
- disorganization;
- risk-taking;
- obsessive thoughts;
- paranoia;
- hopelessness;
- pessimism about the future;
- inability to function; or
- suicidal thinking.

For bipolars without professional treatment, *manic* periods will become more severe, leading to an *increase* in damaging manic symptoms. They might be described as:

- extremely energetic;
- over-committed;
- the life of the party;
- having racing, obsessive thoughts;
- talking excessively loud and rapidly;
- experiencing temper explosions;
- needing little sleep;
- overly optimistic;
- extremely self-confident;
- all-knowing;
- argumentative;
- aggressive and controlling;
- verbally and/or physically abusive;
- addicted to things like alcohol, drugs, gambling, spending, sex, or food;
- financially irresponsible; or
- likely to take extreme risks.

A non-treated bipolar spouse wreaks emotional havoc in the marriage and with the children. Think about these distressing situations:

A bipolar husband left his wife and was living with another woman, but he still wanted to come "home" to eat, sleep, and be with the kids.

A bipolar wife was so strung out on drugs and alcohol that she couldn't be safely trusted to drive the kids to and from school and other activities.

A bipolar husband kept gambling away the family's savings until they were in danger of losing their home.

But there is hope! *Mental Illness and Your Marriage* specifically addresses how bipolar disorder affects a marriage, and how a marriage can be rescued from manic and depressive mood swings.

While this book focuses on marriage repair and enrichment with a bipolar spouse, these same marriage recovery principles will work for marriages affected by most other mental disorders. They will even work for most marriages *not* impacted by mental illness.

Can you relate to the following comments from two frustrated spouses who are ready to give up on their marriages?

A teary wife grimaces, "My husband's mental illness wasn't the sole *cause* of our marital problems. He and I had strains on our relationship long before his bipolar diagnosis. We probably had more friction in our marriage than most of our friends, yet we loved each other and somehow managed to endure our differences.

But ever since he had his breakdown, our relationship's been fragile at best. He's thin skinned, easily agitated, and quickly hurt by me and others. Our kids and

I constantly have to walk on eggshells around him, always afraid we'll say or do something that will trigger an upset. Can he change? Can our marriage be fixed, or should I drop all my expectations and file for divorce?"

An angry husband laments, "My wife's mental disorder has really changed her—and our relationship. Gone is her gentle, sensitive, caring, engaging side. For several years now, she's alternated between totally isolating from everyone and exploding at them in angry outbursts. I've tried everything I know to fix things between us. At times she's just impossible to live with. Is there any chance she'll come around and be her old self again? Or should I face the hard facts and call it quits on our marriage?"

Can you identify with some of these frustrations? If so, this book will give you hope and workable tools to manage your tough reality and rehabilitate your marriage.

2

WHAT ARE YOUR PERSONAL STORIES?

The problem with baggage is that it affects other people's trips.
Chris Hodges

In every marriage, both the husband and wife bring their own problems into their new relationship: life's past wounds, unmet expectations, misplaced priorities, and countless other issues. Because of this marital reality, life coach Rob Liano suggests, "Everyone has baggage. Maybe we should help each other carry it." We both brought lots of baggage into our marriage—here are our stories.

JIM, WHAT'S YOUR STORY?

Many people diagnosed with a mental illness come from happy, well-adjusted homes—I did not. I grew up in a home where my parents fought constantly. My father was an economics professor at Penn State University. My mother, a schoolteacher, suffered from severe and chronic mental illness.

My mom left our family at least eighteen times before I was twenty-one. Much of the time I never knew where she'd gone, or if she'd ever come back, and I often worried that she would commit suicide. She usually blamed my father and me for her leaving. Even when she didn't, I often blamed myself. The guilt, resentment, and fear caused constant inner torment.

Starting at about age four, my mother and maternal grandmother sexually molested me. In seventh grade, I developed bulimia, an eating disorder, to control the weight that I'd gained following the worst times of sexual exploitation.

In college, I participated in three sports: football, wrestling, and boxing. Through the influence of the Fellowship of Christian Athletes, I became a follower of Jesus Christ while I was at the University of Pittsburgh. While in college, I worked with teenage gangs in New York City's Harlem and Lower East Side, coached semi-pro football, and did social work.

I then transferred to Miami University in Oxford, Ohio, where I met Leah on a blind date in the fall of 1964. Like most courting couples, we discussed all sorts of topics, including hobbies, home backgrounds, marriage expectations, parenting roles, faith, and others. We were convinced we knew each other inside and out. I certainly believed Leah was the perfect soul mate for me, and I saw only a bright future for us.

After graduating, I enrolled at Gordon-Conwell Theological Seminary. During my time there, I worked with teenagers and students at Harvard, MIT, and other universities. I also served for half a year in the Danvers

State Mental Hospital as the student chaplain to the Men's Violent Ward.

After graduating from seminary, I went on to pastor in five churches around the country, working in Florida, Texas, Pennsylvania, and California. My last full-time pastoral position was at a church in Newport Beach, California, with a congregation of over 3,000 members.

In 1988, having been in Newport Beach for two years, everything seemed to be going great in my ministry.

Eventually I faced a couple of seemingly minor problems at work, which, in normal circumstances, would not have become a major issue. But, when combined with all the home distress I'd suffered during my childhood years, as well as the recent memories of unfair, brutal treatment by a few members in the three prior churches I'd served at, these work struggles threw me into a mental breakdown.

Although I still managed to carry out my professional duties in the church, I grew severely depressed and suicidal. I started seeing a psychologist and psychiatrist. But even in the midst of my productive, vibrant church ministry, and with the help of counseling and medications, my condition worsened.

I voluntarily entered the psychiatric unit of a local hospital for what I thought would be a weekend of rest and recovery. Five months later, I walked out with a diagnosis of "severe depression."

After a month at home, and still feeling mentally unstable, I decided to try a different mental hospital about an hour from home. Hospitalized there for about three weeks, I was diagnosed with "manic-depressive illness" (now known as bipolar disorder). Later on, that conclusion was updated to "ultra-rapid cycling bipolar disorder," which meant that sometimes I could have radical mood swings up to a dozen times a day.

Since my breakdown, I've been on fifty different psychiatric medications, trying most of them several different times to see if they might finally work the second or third time around. I could have died on six occasions due to pharmacy or physician errors. For my own safety from medications and their side effects, and as a result of dangerous medicine mistakes, I began to read voraciously about psychiatric medications.

In addition to navigating through the mental health system and suffering nearly constant medication problems, I had frequent conflicts with my church denomination's insurance company over its psychiatric coverage.

Needless to say, these ongoing struggles were extremely stressful for Leah and me, and our marriage suffered. We tried to keep these worries from our two young sons, but we couldn't hide our problems from them and they suffered too.

LEAH, WHAT'S YOUR STORY?

I grew up in the 1950s in what outwardly appeared to be a very close, harmonious family: a mom and dad who loved each other, and an obedient son and daughter. To others, our household looked like the ideal family.

My parents grew up in an environment where their feelings were not shared, or even acknowledged, and they continued that tradition in our family.

In my home life, revealing *any* kind of feeling—happiness, anger, fear, frustration, or anything—was almost non-existent.

I knew my parents loved me. They provided what I needed, physically. Both Mom and Dad were concerned and compassionate when I was sick. They also met *some* emotional needs. We laughed together over TV shows and conversations. Bed time meant reading stories and saying prayers. I felt safe and secure in my younger years.

When my younger brother or I acted badly, we were spanked appropriately. But all was forgiven and harmony was restored.

Things seemed to change when I grew older. Looking back, I can see that as I entered adolescence, my father didn't know how to handle my growing up. To cope, he emotionally detached himself from me.

Sometimes Dad wouldn't talk to me, and he came across as cold and distant. I would agonize that I had done something wrong, and when I would apologize all seemed well again.

But to me, this new distance between us signaled that I'd somehow messed things up. I began to feel I had to earn his love and approval in the only way I knew how: by good behavior and good grades.

Since I felt I had to perform to gain my parents' love and approval, I often felt I was less than adequate. Peer pressure in school added to these insecurities. Any success I had was minimized or barely acknowledged. After sharing an accomplishment, I nearly always walked away feeling that what I had done wasn't good enough.

Because my father didn't know how to process his anger and disappointment, he often gave me the silent treatment, which communicated to me that I wasn't good enough, or that there was something wrong with me.

Because my parents couldn't recognize or acknowledge their own inner feelings, I also learned to suppress mine. It took me years to understand and identify what my feelings really were, and even longer to learn how to deal with them.

Later, during college, I met Jim on a blind date. I was intrigued that he was going to study for the ministry. Even though I loved God and thought I had a strong faith, I could tell he had something I didn't have, and I wanted it.

Finally, after reading about the cross of Christ, and that Jesus had died for me personally, I was able to understand God's *personal* love and acceptance of me, and I became a follower of him.

Jim and I were excited about serving Christ together. I graduated from college and we were married on June 24, 1967 of that same year.

Full of early marriage bliss, we were convinced that we knew each other inside and out. Everything seemed great until we'd been married a couple of months. One afternoon Jim got angry at our landlady's behavior and put his fist through our apartment door. I thought, "Whoops, I guess there's more to know about Jim than I thought." I'd just found out the meaning of the phrase, "Love is blind; marriage is the eye-opener!"

I began to observe Jim's mood swings, withdrawals, silent treatments, and angry episodes, and I started noticing patterns.

He is a tremendously driven person with great vision and talent. He would charge into a church and have all kinds of great ideas about where to start. He would just push, push, push until he'd accomplished what he'd set out to do.

Often, after achieving his goals, he'd experience an emotional crash. At first, I thought was just a natural letdown after the adrenaline rush of a major achievement, but in reality it was a situation where he needed some time off. I don't think he knew how to give himself permission to take a break, or how to explain to me his need for some solitary time to unwind.

In these circumstances, I seemed to be the only safe person he could vent to, or pick a fight with. So following a hard energy push and the subsequent letdown, he would often start a fight with me because I'd somehow done something "wrong."

He would use that "issue" to justify taking off for a few days of what he called "R&R," which I called "pouting." He'd leave early in the morning and come home late at night. He would give me the silent treatment, sometimes for days. But after a while he'd feel better, be ready to kiss and make up, and want to move ahead.

Whenever Jim gave me the silent treatment, it dredged up old, painful memories of rejection and insecurity from my family. His actions and attitude left me holding a basket of unresolved self-blame and resentment. Over the years, this behavior became a very corrosive pattern in our relationship and set us up for some serious trouble.

When we came out to California to begin our work in a new church, we knew our marriage was in rough shape. We started marriage therapy, and were soon told we needed individual counseling, which we both started. During this period, Jim suffered his major meltdown.

3

HOW HAS BIPOLAR DISORDER AFFECTED YOUR MARRIAGE?

*When an affliction happens to you, you either let it defeat you,
or you defeat it.*
Jean-Jacques Rousseau

Sometimes marriages fail suddenly due to an unexpected physical or mental illness, an act of unfaithfulness, or some other dramatic event. But most marriages die a slow death.

It's usually the little things in a marriage that pile up, accumulating until their pain becomes unbearable. These seemingly minor "issues" can be like a small pebble in your shoe: For the first half mile of walking, the discomfort is hardly noticeable. But after a mile or two, that tiny pebble becomes an excruciating stone that makes every step painful.

Many marriage coaches observe that couples who are still together don't necessarily have *fewer* adversities. They remain married because they've developed ways to cope with or overcome snags *before* the problems get out of control.

For more than thirty years, we lived with some unhealthy patterns in our relationship. While it's certainly true that Jim's bipolar disorder added terrible pressures and uncertainties to our marriage, we have learned that a mental illness is seldom the sole culprit in an ailing marriage. There are almost always *other* factors that have been at work in unraveling a relationship—the mental disorder just adds to the marital stresses.

JIM, HOW HAS YOUR BIPOLAR DISORDER AFFECTED YOUR MARRIAGE?

My mental illness has produced several negative results that have plagued our marriage: my self-esteem was slashed, my moods caused my family and me to live in a constant state of unsteadiness, and my depressive isolations alienated me from family and friends.

My self-esteem was damaged, and it tainted my relationships. Due to an unhealthy, unstable family background, I grew up with a negative self-image. Fortunately, athletic successes enabled me to use sports accomplishments as a crutch to help me feel better about myself. But when I had my mental crash in 1988 and became suicidal, I could no longer keep up my mostly positive front.

For the twenty years prior to my breakdown, I'd counseled scores of people who were depressed, often including three or four suicidal men every month. Now I became the counselee, the one who had to be hospitalized and attend talk therapy. This shift seriously injured my self-esteem, and in turn hurt my relationship with Leah.

As a result of my hospitalization and mental illness

diagnosis, I felt judged and abandoned. I, who had been a well-regarded professional, became a social leper, an outcast. I, the strong leader, was looked upon by many as a fragile, unreliable "sicko." Some friends never answered my calls. Fellow pastors seldom returned my phone calls and rarely initiated any conversations with me. I, who'd been a respected pastor, was soon blamed and shamed for numerous spiritual shortcomings that "caused" my bipolar condition. Accusations and "sermons" from lay leaders and clergy stung me:

> Jim, your problem is simply that you never could say "no." You just bit off more than you could chew. . . . Maybe you're demon possessed. Why don't you come to our exorcism meeting and we'll cast them out . . . Your real issue is some secret personal sin that's in your life, and you need to repent of it. . . . You don't need shrinks and pills, just have more faith. Trust God. Read your Bible more. . . . Face it, you'll never return to the ministry. You'll never hold a job again because of your bipolar disorder.

These misunderstandings, judgments, and rejections hurt me deeply and eroded my sense of self-worth. I mused:

> What can I do with my life if I can't work as a pastor anymore? Are there any other kinds of work I could do in spite of my current unpredictability? Since I'm on disability, and so many others have lost respect for me, Leah's probably lost her admiration for me as well.

Surely she doesn't love me anymore. Maybe she's planning to leave me.

Those thoughts tapped right into some of my childhood abandonment issues and constantly gnawed away at my relationship with Leah.

My mood changes forced Leah and our sons to live continually off-balance as I see-sawed between serious depression and agitated manias. Within a week, a day, or even an hour, I could go from high-energy productivity and optimism to angry outbursts, isolation from everyone, or even suicidal depression.

I became far more sensitive to hurts from other people, including Leah. When others criticized or rejected me, or if I worked too late at night, it would often set off an agitated mania or a severe depression. Living with me was like tip-toeing through a minefield. Old issues that she and I had previously dealt with often re-surfaced and exploded.

Although I battled mostly with depression, my manias were equally disruptive. In my manic states, I've gone for months on less than two or three hours of sleep a night. But even in shorter durations of mania, I became ultra-talkative, easily angered, and excessively argumentative. Leah says my manias were harder on her than my depressions.

These constant ups and downs left my family and I riddled with anxiety, edginess, resentment, and fear. Because of this, we were never able to establish a safe rhythm in life and never knew what to expect. There was no stability.

My depressive isolations cut me off from family

and friends. Oftentimes I would leave the house because I didn't want my family to see me in one of my upsetting moods. I was always worried that I might say or do something that I might later regret. Those absences and erratic moods caused a lot of collateral damage to Leah and our sons, and I missed out on a lot of life's important moments.

LEAH, HOW HAS JIM'S BIPOLAR DISORDER AFFECTED YOUR MARRIAGE?

All marriages have difficulties, even under the best of circumstances, but it's especially tough when a mental illness is involved. Jim's bipolar illness has negatively disrupted our marriage in a number of ways: I've suffered many painful emotions related to his illness, I've had to adjust to an unpredictable social life, and I've had to live with the reality of Jim's possible suicide.

Because of Jim's temperament and behavior changes, I've suffered my own painful emotions. Emotionally, I didn't have much left for Jim. I had a hard time reconciling the old Jim with the new Jim. Living with him as he battled his moods was, for me, terrifying, frustrating, and anger-inducing. I eventually realized that his treatment of me was verbally and emotionally abusive.

My feelings of love for and trust in him were gone. I often worried, "What is our future together going to look like?" Many times, we grieved the loss of what we'd had in our relationship when things were better. During this time, Jim and I both went through scary feelings of intense anxiety, mistrust of each other, and dreads of abandonment.

Billy Graham's wife, Ruth, was once asked, "Having

been married as long as you and your husband have, you've must have had your share of differences over the years. Have you ever considered divorce?" Ruth responded, "Divorce, no. Murder, yes!" I can certainly relate.

I often grew very frustrated with Jim's inability to do simple tasks. Because of his medications, he had problems with concentrating and remembering. Filling out simple forms, especially insurance forms or applications, was difficult for him. He had always had a tendency to lose things, but it became much worse after being on psychiatric medications.

It angered me that Jim was not troubled by the reality that he had such a short fuse—that he was so easily angered, overwhelmed, frustrated, disturbed. What many people don't realize is that manic times are as devastating as depressive ones, if not worse. His mood swings were extremely difficult on me and our boys. I had to be continually on guard not to say or do something that might set him off.

With the progress we've made, these swings happen much less often. Yet even now, when I come home from work and walk into the house, I'm still not quite sure what I'll find. I tense up until I figure out where Jim is emotionally. I can be met by the gray cloud of his depression, or the agitated tension and boundless energy of his mania. Sometimes I come home and he is "normal"—in that nice, comfortable, "middle" mood. And that makes it a good day.

I've had to adjust to a fragile, unpredictable social life. Although Jim's mood shifts became more predictable due to medication and counseling, I often had to remind myself that socializing might never be like it used to be. This was and is our "new normal:" a social life with limited predictability.

It's very difficult to plan get-togethers with others because I don't know what kind of mood Jim's going to be in. I'm never quite sure whether or not he's going to be able to attend a social event with friends or a church function. When he is able to go, we make the best of it, but sometimes we have to cancel or I go by myself.

I've had to live with the fear of Jim's possible suicide. The suicide statistics for people living with bipolar disorder are sobering: nearly half of bipolars try to kill themselves, and one in five completes the suicide.

This precarious state put a lot of stress on me. Often, during Jim's most fragile stretches, I felt edgy, frustrated, fearful, and angry. But despite feeling totally helpless, I felt like I had to at least do something.

I knew that many lives have been saved by putting a suicidal person on a psychiatric hold in a mental facility for 72 hours. So at first, I considered calling 911 to have the police forcibly take Jim to a mental facility.

But I resisted this choice because of Jim's previous experience in mental hospitals. As a patient, he'd been frequently intimidated by the insurance company to leave the institution prematurely, against his medical team's advice. The insurance people repeatedly warned that they could have him forcibly discharged against his doctors' orders and that they could drop their coverage, leaving his family responsible for all the bills.

These injustices left Jim utterly determined to never again be hospitalized and forced to endure similar threats. He made it clear that rather than having to once again suffer such turmoil, he would end his life—in or out of a hospital.

Instead of subjecting Jim to the extra pressure of a mental hospital, I chose to pray for Jim's safety, surrender him to God's care, and confide with a trusted friend. I had to accept the fact that I couldn't "fix" Jim—only God could do that. I had to turn Jim over to God, to protect him from harming himself.

4

HOW HAVE YOU COPED WITH THE EFFECTS OF BIPOLAR DISORDER?

In every marriage more than a week old, there are grounds for divorce. The trick is to find, and continue to find, grounds for marriage.
Robert Anderson

The key to successfully handling the effects of bipolar disorder starts with accepting the harsh reality of your illness. The sooner you can do this, the sooner you can begin to cope effectively with your struggles and move forward.

Michael J. Fox noted that "acceptance doesn't mean resignation: it means understanding that something is what it is and there's got to be a way through it." He explained, "My happiness grows in direct proportion to my acceptance, and in inverse proportion to my expectations."

JIM, HOW HAVE YOU COPED WITH THE EFFECTS OF BIPOLAR DISORDER?

I desperately wanted to get better, mostly for my family's sake, and was willing to go to any length to reclaim my life. I longed to be the husband and father they deserved. Through all the years of struggle, I discovered, and still use, a variety of techniques to help me cope with my mood issues.

I studied literature on recovery and spiritual development. I studied material from Alcoholics Anonymous and other 12-step groups to gain insights into how to deal with personal struggles, relationships, and marriage.

The Bible is obviously a great place to start for spiritual development. Sure, there were times when I couldn't get myself to read the Bible, or even pray. But the Bible has been my strongest spiritual support all along. It's given me hope and guidance, and among other things it's supplied incredible practical help for my relationship with Leah.

I searched for supportive people and sought out relationships and friendships. During the first few years after my hospitalization, I experienced frequent episodes of depression and mania. These terrible bouts often caused me to withdraw from people, both friends and acquaintances. For several years, I had to cancel half my appointments due to my ever-changing moods. Sometimes I didn't answer phone calls for weeks or even months.

One of the findings of the book *The Friendless American Male* is that the vast majority of all American men do not have a single friend whom they feel comfortable and safe enough to call at 2 a.m. for help.

I'd read *The Friendless American Male* some years prior to my breakdown, and I was acutely aware of the necessity of men having a few reliable friends. Although I had many so-called friends and co-workers, I knew that in reality I, too, had become a "friendless American male." In my plight, I knew that I'd never recover alone. I needed others if I was going to get better and stay better.

With this in mind, I forced myself to develop a support system. It was risky and I chanced getting hurtful comments. Yet I forced myself to meet with three or four trusted friends on a weekly basis. I reconnected with an old best friend and talked regularly with him by long distance phone. I met weekly with my psychologist, who became not only a guide, but a dear friend and mentor.

I attended support groups. For many years, I have participated in 12-step groups at least once or twice a week. One was a group of men who had been sexually abused and had all kinds of addiction issues and mental disorders.

Although I've never had any kind of alcohol problem, I have attended countless Alcoholics Anonymous and other 12-step meetings since 1990. I found the sharing of my own struggles as well as listening to those of others to be encouraging and freeing.

At an AA meeting, I simply introduced myself by saying, "I'm Jim. I'm an addict." This was certainly true as I was a recovering bulimic and am still a food addict. In these meetings, I picked up countless recovery tips for dealing with my bipolar and eating issues. These gatherings provided a degree of anonymity for me, and I felt safe to share without risking criticism, being sermonized to, or gossiped about. Sadly I hadn't found this kind of rugged, caring honesty in most church communities.

Another support group I was involved with was Comfort Zone, a mental illness support group that a therapist and I started over twenty-five years ago, and which continues to meet to this day.

I took personal responsibility for my actions. The Alcoholics Anonymous's tenth step toward sobriety says, "[We] continued to take personal inventory and when we were wrong promptly admitted it." I stopped blaming others, and I learned to accept responsibility for my own harmful attitudes, words, and behaviors.

In the past, when I was in an agitated, fuming, manic mood, I would rationalize my hurtful actions. It was easier to blame somebody or something else than to choose to "own-up" and take charge of making better decisions.

As I learned more about the teachings of Alcoholics Anonymous, I started putting its lessons into practice with my struggles, my relationships, and especially with Leah. As I practiced these principles with her, I had to eat a lot of "humble pie." Whenever I messed up with Leah, I began to promptly admit my wrong. I started saying things like, "Honey, I was in a bad place yesterday. But no matter whether the medication started it, or the stress set me off in a manic or depressive episode, I was still responsible for managing it. And I'm sorry I hurt you."

Putting this teaching from Alcoholics Anonymous into practice has made a huge difference in our relationship. When I admitted I was wrong, it helped Leah process the hurt I'd caused and helped her begin to forgive me.

To my surprise and gratitude, Leah also quickly began

to own up in matters that affected me by promptly admitting her own wrongs.

We discovered that our quick admission of wrongdoing diffused potential buildups of resentments and prevented many misunderstandings and hurt feelings. The simple act of admitting a wrong became a healing, reconciling step that produced countless positives in our relationship.

I learned to identify my triggers for relapses. From my 12-step reading and group meetings, I discovered how to identify what set off my manias and depressions. I found that my triggers were: getting overwhelmed by my workload; toiling too many hours at too fast a pace; having unrealistic expectations of myself or others; being disappointed, criticized, or rejected; and going with too little sleep.

As I discerned my specific causes for relapses, I shared them with Leah so she could alert me when she sensed I was skating on thin ice.

I picked up ways to protect myself from unnecessarily harsh criticisms. This meant avoiding specific people, leaving an event when things grew too toxic, or even avoiding certain gatherings in the first place.

As a leader, it was fairly common to receive a few critical remarks at social gatherings, parties, or church events. Sometimes church people can be hurtful without knowing it. Or, in some instances, they can be deliberately vicious. Often, when I felt uncomfortable with others' comments, I'd get away from an activity, isolating myself by taking a drive or going to a movie, lest I say something that might lead to serious consequences.

I learned how and when to detach. Like most

couples, Leah and I had our share of friction in our relationship. This included things like bringing up past hurts the other had caused, using ill-chosen words, or disagreements on issues such as: expectations of each other, finances, parenting, sex, social obligations, and other flash points.

Until I learned techniques to detach from Leah in healthy ways, I stumbled along as best I could. I tried to protect both myself and her from overreacting to an issue. I realized that if I didn't act quickly and do something *proactive*, my emotions might spin out of control and end with abusive damages to her.

Sometimes, when trying to avoid an argument with Leah, I'd detach from her by giving her the silent treatment, sometimes to punish her, other times simply to protect myself from her words. Of course, I didn't want to admit to myself how cruel my silences were, but I knew how much they hurt her and I worked hard to stop.

Eventually, I learned healthier ways to detach from Leah. I'd say something like, "I'm really upset right now, and I don't want to talk about it because I'm afraid I'll say something I might later regret. I need to cool down and rethink this. Let's discuss this matter tomorrow," or, "I need some time and space to think about this, so I'm going for a drive. Please don't take my absence as a silent treatment."

To disengage, sometimes I'd say to myself, "That's *her* problem this time. It's not about me. She's dealing with her *own* issue. Even if I caused her upset, I can't do anything about it other than to apologize."

If I was upset about something or somebody other than Leah, I'd tell her, "I'm in a bad mood right now. I need to get away so I can calm down and mentally evaluate what's going on to see how I can better deal with it. My withdrawal has nothing to do with you. I'm just trying to take care of myself."

I learned the therapeutic value of writing. When upset, I'd frequently write about my raw emotions and what I thought caused them. I visited different 24-hour restaurants and wrote on napkins and paper placemats about whatever recent altercation I was having with Leah or someone else. Surprisingly, this simple exercise helped me process my emotions, giving me more objectivity and added perspective on my distresses.

I used the Serenity Prayer to cope. The complete prayer, attributed to Reinhold Niebuhr, is used by most 12-step group members:

> God, grant me serenity to accept the things I cannot change, courage to change the things I can, and wisdom to know the difference; living one day at a time, enjoying one moment at a time; accepting hardship as a pathway to peace; taking, as Jesus did, this sinful world as it is, not as I would have it; trusting that you will make all things right if I surrender to your will, so that I may be reasonably happy in this life and supremely happy with you in the next. Amen.

Yet, as helpful as this prayer was in reassuring me, there were also times when I just couldn't pray it because I was too sulky or depressed.

For instance, once in a while Leah would say or do something that really rubbed me the wrong way. She may have listened to my sharing in a rushed, impatient manner and been ultra-quick to give advice, which I would take as being a judgmental "sermon." Or maybe she'd side with the person who was upsetting me.

My knee-jerk reaction would be to snap at Leah, criticizing her actions. But when I prayed the full Serenity Prayer and applied its concepts to my relationship with her, I was able to accept Leah as she was: a person just trying to cope with our tough situation. This freed me to stop my attempts at changing or fixing her. Invoking the Serenity Prayer shifted my attention so I could focus on changing my *own* negative attitudes and destructive responses.

In Alcoholics Anonymous, they call it "letting go and letting God." As I tried to apply that slogan to my own situation, I would turn Leah and our dispute over to God and say to him, "I blew it, please help me pick up the pieces. I'll trust you to guide me as I work on this strain in Leah's and my relationship."

I learned to forgive myself and Leah. Ruth Bell Graham says that "A happy marriage is the union of two good forgivers." Both Leah and I agree. I've had to forgive myself for my own mess-ups. And I also had to forgive Leah when she'd hurt me by her angry words of frustration, or when she made time with me a low priority in her relationships.

Reading the Bible and other inspirational literature such as Dr. Lewis Smedes's book *Forgive & Forget: Healing the Hurts We Don't Deserve* helped me understand what forgiveness is and is not, as well as healthy ways to begin forgiving. I discovered that if I didn't forgive Leah and others for some of the hurtful things they'd said or done, I'd become a prisoner to my past—always rehearsing the litany of wrongs done to me, always thinking of ways to get even.

His words offered solid guidance and freed me to allow for my failures at forgiving—pardoning one day then resenting on the next. I learned that forgiving is a process, and no one gets it right all the time.

Smedes's book awakened me to the damage that could come to me and my relationship with Leah if I didn't at least *want* to start forgiving.

LEAH, HOW HAVE YOU COPED WITH THE EFFECTS OF JIM'S BIPOLAR DISORDER?

Jim frequently says that education is over half the battle in dealing with bipolar disorder or other brain illnesses. I agree with him, because I believe knowledge about an illness and its treatments is as necessary for family members as it is for patients.

Although I'd taken some counseling courses while in seminary, I was pretty much in the dark when it came to knowledge about mental illness and bipolar disorder.

Initially, it was hard for me to tell the difference between the real Jim and the Jim with the bipolar condition. Gradually, I learned information about his mind disorder through reading, attending mental illness conferences, and talking with therapists, psychiatrists, and patients and their family members.

And, unexpectedly, I probably got my *best* education from *Jim*—through his sharing about it. At times, his explanations came in manic rambles, but they were very helpful nevertheless. Plus, I also observed him in different situations and began to actually see how stresses, medications, and their side effects affected him.

I learned to forgive myself and Jim. A strong, vibrant marriage is a *two-way* street. It was important to realize that *both* of us needed to work on forgiveness.

In western movies, good guys and bad guys are easy to distinguish: the bad cowboy always wears a black hat and the good cowboy wears a white one. Let's face it: in our marriage, Jim doesn't always wear the black hat and I don't always wear the white hat. He's not the bad guy and I'm not the good guy in our relationship—we both bring negatives and positives into our marriage.

I have to be responsible for dealing with my own issues and the things in my life that need to be changed. Sometimes this means saying, "I'm sorry I hurt you, Jim. I was wrong." And when he does the same, I need to be willing to forgive him.

I saw our marriage as a lifelong commitment. The pastor and theologian Dietrich Bonhoeffer wrote to a young bride and groom from his prison cell in Nazi Germany in 1943. He told them, "It is not your *love* that sustains your marriage, but from now on, your *marriage* will sustain your love." (emphasis ours)

We agree with Bonhoeffer that it's not romantic feelings that will keep your marriage together. Rather, it's your commitment to your *marriage and its vows* that will keep your love together. This has certainly been true for us—and it's still true for couples in today's world!

We took very seriously the vows we made on June 24, 1967: "For better or for worse." Believe me, it got worse for us. Many times. But we've also made it better.

You wedding vows, your duty, and your stubborn

loyalty to your partner will be one of the key things holding your marriage together.

Reminding yourself often of the importance of your "for better or worse" commitment to each other will help you to hang in there until feelings of love return. This will act like an anchor for your relationship in the midst of bitter, long-lasting storms. Although, I jokingly admit that at times our relationship could be described the way singers Simon and Garfunkel described theirs: "We've had many fights over the years, but we no longer fight. We're just too exhausted!"

I separated Jim from his illness. During the first seven or eight years after his hospitalization, Jim wasn't his old self. Sometimes Jim was so overly medicated he could barely function. At other times, his medications were either not working, or were actually causing some of his manias or depressions. Plus, he was facing severe conflicts with our denomination's insurance company and still knew very little about "recovery tools."

Our sons were young then, and things were pretty tough for all of us. The boys and I would get together and vent. They'd complain, "Why can't Dad stop talking so much. I can't stand it when he wants me to get things for him all the time, and I feel like a slave waiting on him. Why does he sleep all day? Why won't he answer the phone or help with house chores?"

Unloading and getting it all out was a good thing. But then I'd always try to remind them, "Remember, that's not your real Dad when he acts like he does—it is his illness or medications that are affecting him. Let's try to remember who Dad really is beneath his frustrating behaviors." Easier said than done, but it was important for me and our boys to separate Jim's bipolar symptoms from the real Jim.

I found safe, supportive friends. Like Jim, I have developed a group of friends with whom I can safely vent. I can swear, spit, stomp, or cry when I need to, and I know that they won't bail on me, or Jim. This last point is very important; they'll still support him and be his friend because they understand it's his illness that affects our marriage, not just his own rough edges.

I learned how to emotionally detach from Jim. In my counseling, I learned that I had to come to grips with my co-dependent issues. The best thing I ever learned was that I could not fix Jim—all I could do was control and repair myself.

I realized I couldn't go up and down with Jim's highs and lows. It was emotionally impossible and would drive me crazy trying to do it. I had to keep functioning at a normal, steady pace to keep our family together. I still tried to be sympathetic to Jim's upheavals, but there was no way I could truly understand his feelings. By letting go of the need to become deeply empathetic with his ever-changing moods, I freed myself to become emotionally healthy.

I resigned as Jim's caregiver. I had to surrender all attempts to "mother" Jim. I encouraged him to be totally responsible for managing every aspect of his illness. Jim took full responsibility for all of his appointments and for how he managed his day. He, not I, was in control of his medications, counseling, and support group attendance. I still try to encourage him as best I can, complimenting him in his attempts and accomplishments, but I've learned to stay out of it and let him make all his own decisions.

I learned how to set boundaries. Through my experiences with Jim, I've learned that unless a mentally ill person is in a psychotic state and out of touch with reality, he or she can respond to upsets in a civil manner if firm boundaries are set.

Early on, when things were extremely chaotic, I had to set some protective financial boundaries. I cancelled some credit cards and changed some bank accounts to protect our family from a possible manic-induced reckless spending spree.

After a lot of turbulent years, I learned how to create boundaries. My boundary setting (and maintaining) became a way to protect myself against the verbal and emotional abuse that sometimes could come with bouts of Jim's manic agitations or rages.

If he started getting out of hand with anger, or swearing, or yelling, I'd say something like, "Jim, I know you're upset and you have every right to be. But I'm not going to listen to this tone of voice, and so when you can calm down we can discuss this civilly. But until then, please leave the room, or I will."

It wasn't easy to do that. It took me a long time to be comfortable setting limits on what behavior and words I would or would not accept, but the effort was worth it.

Boundary setting takes experimenting and courage, but it's vital for both you and your spouse. Your limits may not involve abusive words or behavior. They can cover such areas as spending, house chores, drinking, drug use, and others sources of conflict.

I learned the importance of timing. When coping with a loved one's emotional struggles, it is very important to know *when* to communicate.

There is a lot of irrational thinking going on in a bipolar person's mania or depression. It helped me to understand that Jim's moods dictated how and when I communicated with him.

Trying to have a rational, meaningful discussion when a bipolar person is in a psychotic state is nearly impossible.

When that person is manic, it is useless—he or she is too argumentative, agitated, all-knowing, or easily distracted. Having a sensible conversation when your loved one is really manic will be like spitting into the wind. Because of this reality, when Jim was in a manic period, our conversations had to be very limited.

I found that attempting to converse meaningfully with Jim when he was manic was frustrating—and a waste of time. Often, I had to wait until he dropped into a depressed or "neutral" state—when he'd be open to talking without being extra-argumentative or stringing together unrelated topics.

Having a meaningful conversation with a depressed individual can be more fruitful than one who's manic, but most depressed people don't want to talk much. If Jim was badly depressed, he'd shut down and avoid interactions with me or anyone else.

I discovered that sometimes I had no other option but to wait until Jim got somewhere into the middle ground before we could have a productive conversation about feelings or decisions that had to be made. It made all the difference in the world when he was able to hone in and concentrate on a conversation.

I found a new career role for my life. I had to move on with my life, to recharge my emotional batteries from the constant draining of Jim's ups and downs. Without Jim's normal income, and now limited to his monthly disability checks, my salary wasn't enough to support our family's needs and Jim's growing medical and counseling bills. I needed to find more meaningful, better-paying work.

For our first two years in California, I worked as an elementary school teacher at a small, nearby Christian school. I enjoyed the work, but teaching had its share of stresses, and the salary was modest. I had to find other employment that could help us better financially. To increase my salary, I worked for the next few years as a secretary in a large company, then took a position as a school secretary.

I liked my elementary teaching and secretarial work, but something was missing. I needed something more fulfilling. I wanted to work directly with people in a spiritual context, doing counseling, speaking, and organizing. So I started on what would be a ten-year journey that finished with me being ordained as a minister.

In 1991, while still working full time, I began taking one class per quarter at Fuller Theological Seminary. Even though I wasn't sure where or how I'd ultimately use that seminary education, I stuck with my studies.

The courses really resonated with me. They opened my eyes to the possibility of some kind of full-time professional ministry similar to what I was doing part time at my Newport Beach church. All along, Jim was extremely supportive of my academic program and new career direction.

Then, in 1993, the senior minister of St. Andrews Presbyterian Church, where my husband had served, offered me a part time position on its staff as visitation minister. I was thrilled! For the next ten years, it enabled me to earn enough income to meet our family's basic needs, plus get practical experience in ministry and continue my part time studies at Fuller.

I finally graduated from Fuller Seminary in 2001 with a Masters of Divinity, and I went to work full time on the church's staff with an expanded job description as minister of congregational care. For me, seminary education was a huge help in separating from Jim's problems and moving ahead with my life.

I made it a priority to keep my own emotional gas tank full. I believe it's important for those of us living with a spouse who has a mental illness to find things that fill us, encourage us, and make us want to move on and enjoy life. These may be leisure pursuits, a new career, or volunteer work.

If I burned out with caregiving, or got depressed over my situation, Jim and our sons would suffer. So I had to push myself to do things that were fun, meaningful, and distracting from my daily pressures: regular exercise, movies, concerts, phone conversations with friends, and other positive activities.

For you, finding emotional fulfillment may not mean a career or education change. It might be experimenting with a new interest, or taking some community college courses you've always been interested in. But you've got to do something to fill your own gas tank and have something that you look forward to doing.

5

WHAT HAVE YOU DONE TO HEAL YOUR MARRIAGE?

*Our greatest weakness lies in giving up. The most certain way
to succeed is always to try just one more time.*
Thomas Edison

Restoring an injured marriage starts with a deliberate choice to begin again and again and again. As a couple works at rebuilding their strained marital relationship, it takes rugged willingness and patient endurance. Sometimes, the healthy partner must give 99 percent of the effort because the other may be unable due to an emotional or physical disability.

While this is certainly tough, it's often the only way to heal a marriage struggling with the effects of mental illness, and as things improve, the effort will become more balanced.

JIM, WHAT HAVE YOU DONE TO HEAL YOUR MARRIAGE?

I realized pretty quickly that I'd have to take personal responsibility for healing our marriage. Although I have messed up plenty of times, I've worked really hard to heal and rebuild our relationship.

I initiated daily communication about our feelings. We share our highs and lows, and how we feel about them. This helps us communicate on an emotional rather than factual level. I wanted to avoid simply swapping a rambling list of activities we'd done that day, saying, "I did this and I did that." Most of the time we do this while at the dinner table or after dinner while sitting on the family room sofa. We try to communicate this way nearly every day.

I made time for weekly dates. When you have a young family, it's tough to afford the babysitting and other date expenses. But we discovered that we couldn't afford *not* to have some kind of date each week. It can be any kind of easy, fun activity where we could be alone together without our sons or anyone else. Sometimes our date is as simple as zoning out at a movie or taking our dog for a walk on the beach.

Of course, we've occasionally had to skip our date times due to life's interruptions. Yet, for most of our married life, we've tried to have weekly dates. Just getting out of the house and away from phone calls, household tasks, other people—even our sons—always brings a welcome change of pace.

I injected surprises and humor into our relationship. I used, and still use, laughter to help relieve Leah's and my stresses. Humor adds levity to serious situations.

A couple of years ago, I surprised her with a date, telling her, "Dress appropriately because we're going to a summer dinner theater."

She was ecstatic and got all dressed up. She looked stunning. I kept our true destination a secret until the very last minute when she finally guessed what I was up to.

The dinner theatre was actually a Los Angeles Angels evening baseball game. As we drove down the freeway exit to get off at the stadium, she growled, "Jim are we going to a baseball game and not a dinner theatre?" I said, "Sure. It's a unique kind of dinner theatre. The ball game will be a 'live performance,' and our dinner will be gorging on peanuts, hot dogs, and soda."

I won't tell you what she said, but her one word, unchristian exclamation said it all! Nevertheless, we actually had a great time and a lot of laughs over the surprise "dinner theatre."

I took Leah on mini honeymoons. Besides weekly dates, I usually initiate taking two or three "mini-moons" a year, when we escape for one or two nights. A mini-vacation furnishes us with a chance to get away and talk without interruptions. These brief getaways help to distance ourselves from the pressures of our daily schedules. My planning takes the burden off of Leah. All she needs to do is pack and enjoy our time away. We check into a hotel and just read a novel, watch TV, catch a couple of movies, take walks, and enjoy meals out together.

I found tools to manage my stress. I realized that when I was frazzled about something, its effects spilled over and also upset Leah. To prevent this, I developed a set of stress-reducing tools. For example, when worried about something, I intentionally distract my negative, obsessive thoughts with activities like movies, sports events, TV, videos, walking our dog, and reading.

I also handle my stresses by writing about them. Putting them on paper doesn't eliminate them, but it helps me slow down and process my racing thoughts, shielding me from their constant mental attacks.

Another anti-stress tool I use is calling friends to sound off when I was anxious, angry, or overwhelmed. All these tools help reduce my nervous tension, and, in turn, reduce Leah's.

I monitored my workload. I wasn't always sure whether it was my Type-A, hard-working personality that made me this way or if it was a burst of manic energy, but I discovered that when I dug in to various tasks, I had a hard time knowing when to stop. To prevent this, I have to keep an eye on my schedule to make sure I'm not over-committed and won't overwork on a project. I pace myself with more breaks, and have learned to flex my self-set deadlines.

If I was pushing too hard or too long, or was feeling overwhelmed by a home task or ministry project, I tended to be irritable, curt, or impatient with Leah and the boys. I noticed that these reactions caused Leah to pull away from me until I cooled down. To protect our marriage, I knew I had to be careful to keep a healthy work-life balance.

I was careful to get enough sleep. There were times when I got wrapped up doing a hobby or work assign-ment and worked late into the night. In my enthusiasms, my mind often refused to shut down when I went to bed.

I learned that for a bipolar person, going with little or no sleep is a clear warning sign that a manic episode is right around the corner. So, before it was too late at night and my mind was off to the races, I made it a habit to shut off my computer—or turn off the TV—to slow my racing thoughts and put me to sleep.

I would make every effort to somehow knock myself out before I stayed up too late or all night. Sometimes I had to experiment, because what worked one time wasn't always effective another time.

Besides getting over-involved in some project or hobby, I occasionally got extremely troubled over some situation and obsessed over it until the wee hours of the morning.

Time and again, lack of sleep set me off into a manic phase which left me easily agitated or depressed and withdrawn. My mania-induced hair-trigger anger sometimes flared up over something Leah said or did. Or my silent moods erected a barrier between us. My responses set off in her unwarranted self-blame, resentment at me, or outright fear. Getting enough sleep helped me prevent this.

I helped with household chores. Due to Leah's long work hours, I try to relieve her from the pressure of doing many home chores by becoming "Mr. Mom" around the house. Since I don't have a mechanical or electronic bone in my body, I am pretty helpless as a handyman. But I am able to do simple things like shopping, cooking meals, doing the dishes, taking the garbage out, vacuuming, and washing the car.

I encouraged and affirmed Leah. I encourage her in little ways by writing her poems, leaving notes for her on her car seat, or by complimenting the way she looks. I try to recognize her accomplishments by praising a talk or sermon she's given, the great job she's done counseling someone, or for her discipline in doing walking exercises with her friends.

I learned as much as I could about rebuilding our marriage. Because I grew up in such a horrific home background and had very inadequate role models, I've needed to learn these skills on my own.

Throughout our married life, and even before my bipolar hospitalization, I committed to educating myself about being a good husband and dad. I did this in several ways: I used "academic" methods like reading books and articles, or by listening to CDs. I observed and copied other men whom I thought were doing it right as husbands or fathers. And I received individual and marriage counseling that provided helpful insights, guidance, and sensitive support. Through these efforts, I've managed to learn much of what my parents weren't able to teach me about healthy relationships.

LEAH, WHAT HAVE YOU DONE TO HEAL YOUR MARRIAGE?

Early on in Jim's illness, I tried and tried everything I knew to help make him better, but nothing seemed to work. His moods still intimidated me. However, through counseling, reading, and talking with family members of mentally ill persons, I finally realized that the only person I could really improve was *me*. My primary responsibility in healing our marriage was not to focus on manipulating, coercing, or pushing Jim to improve—my job was to make appropriate changes in my attitudes and actions.

The Serenity Prayer really helped me grasp this reality: "God grant me the serenity to accept the things I cannot change, courage to change the things I can, and wisdom to know the difference."

I went to professional counseling. After our initial marriage counseling, our therapist suggested that we get individual counseling. Fortunately, we both found excellent therapists.

Through counseling, I discovered how codependent I was. I had thought it was my responsibility to "fix" problems and make everyone around me happy. It brought a huge relief to discover that the only person I could really "fix" was *me*!

Counseling helped in many ways, but the three most important benefits were: a safe place to unload my frustrations, angers, and fears; an understanding of how my childhood issues impacted my current thoughts and emotions; and better coping skills.

When mental illness is involved, Jim and I believe it's important to get professional counseling, both individually and as a couple.

I prayed, both *for* Jim and *with* him. God is central to both Jim and me. Our faith in him through Jesus Christ is really the core of what's kept us going despite our conflicts and wounds. Sharing with each other something from a sermon, the Bible, a book, an article, or a faith-related conversation with someone has helped us grow spiritually together.

Our common trust in God's management over all of life, our relationship, and our individual lives was, and still is, the *key* part of our relationship. We have blessings at meals; we pray for each other's needs, tasks, decisions, and opportunities; and we pray together about our sons and their families, among countless other things.

I chose to reattach to Jim. We could have just gone ahead merely coexisting under the same roof, but we decided we really wanted to heal our marriage and make it the best it could be.

Earlier in the book, I mentioned that I had to emotionally detach from Jim. At the time, that was the right thing to do. But eventually, I had to actually make a deliberate decision to choose to reattach to him so we could try to heal and rebuild our relationship.

Emotionally detaching was a good way to help heal *myself.* But once I was healthy, I had to jump back in to work at healing our marriage. This time, however, I was reattaching not because of co-dependence but because of love.

I must admit that it's still not easy to know how or when it's safe to move ahead and rebuild. It's an ever-changing process, and there are no shortcuts, no easy answers. But reattaching is an active choice that's important to make.

I asked God for help to restore me from my hurt and mistrust. Jim's words and behaviors over the years, both before and after his hospitalizations, had left me with layers of unresolved resentments, self-condemnation, and anxiety. I asked God for his help in restoring my feelings of affection for Jim, and they've slowly come back. At the same time, we gradually rebuilt our trust in one another.

I took up hobbies we both enjoy. Jim is a natural athlete and loves bicycling, so I've also taken up the sport. It's a great low-pressure way to spend time together, and by riding together we can get some exercise and enjoy the fresh air.

We also love to travel and see new places. With Jim retired and me working only three days a week, we have time to travel. Part of our family lives across the country, and we enjoy traveling to visit them. We are blessed with two awesome sons, two super daughters-in-law, and four delightful grandchildren. Any time we can spend with them is pure joy, and visiting them combines our two favorite pastimes: being with family and travel.

I alerted our sons to watch for warning signs of mania or depression. Both boys are aware that there is a chance they may have inherited their father's bipolar illness. Of course, as their parents, both Jim and I are concerned about that.

They understand that if they start to experience any warning signs of mania or depression, they know to get help right away and not let it escalate.

This relieves Jim and me of lots of worries and has given us greater peace in our relationship. Because we've done all we can to prepare our sons for the worst possibility, we've stopped blaming ourselves for somehow putting them at risk.

I worked on my sense of humor. Jim loves practical jokes. It's taken me time to appreciate them, but I'm getting closer, and I'm learning to laugh more. I've begun to see the truth in the saying:

We don't stop laughing
Because we grow old.
We grow old because
We stop laughing.

I've also learned to have a sense of humor about life. Something both Jim and I find amusing are our role reversals. It's really funny when we go to get into bed at night because he's planning what to make for dinner the next day, and I'm thinking about what work meetings I have the next day—quite the opposite of earlier in our marriage.

I developed realistic expectations. I've learned to hold my expectations loosely. If it's a good day, I take it in, enjoy it, and celebrate. And if it's been a bad day, I accept it for what it is, let it go, and move on. It's been forty-nine years since Jim and I were married and twenty-eight years since his bipolar diagnosis. We realize that our relationship will never be all that we dreamed of it becoming, but it's still good, and it's getting better!

6

HOW CAN A COUPLE JUMPSTART THEIR HEALING?

A successful marriage requires falling in love many times,
always with the same person.
Mignon McLaughlin

While there are countless things you can do to repair your marriage, we'll present to you the ones that have worked for us and people we know. You don't need to use them all, just use what works for you.

Some of these strategies involve deepening a relationship with God. While we believe in God, we know that not everybody else does, or maybe not in the same way as we do. No matter what your beliefs, finding strength in a higher power plays an important role in healing. So, whenever we mention God, simply apply these tips to God however you know him.

But first, we recommend that you and your spouse talk through a few questions about how your family backgrounds and life experiences (the good, the bad, and the ugly) have shaped you.

- What are some specific examples of events in your childhood, teenage years, young adulthood, and adult life that are still affecting you—for good or ill?
- In what ways have your parents, siblings, and others positively or negatively influenced each of you and your marriage?
- What can you do to minimize or avoid the negative effects of your past on your marriage?
- What are some good experiences from your past that you can build into your marriage?

Having spent a little time discussing the ways your past could be influencing your present, now it's your turn to begin rebuilding. Here are some action steps you and your spouse can take to start healing your marriage.

IF YOU HAVE A MENTAL ILLNESS:

- Identify any unhealthy patterns of communicating with your partner.
- Determine which specific mental-illness-related behaviors are harming you, your spouse, and your children.
- Implement adjustments that will ensure the best happiness and safety for you, your spouse, and your children.
- Take responsibility for your own recovery.
- Learn all you can about your illness and its treatment and recovery tactics.

- Get professional counseling for you, your spouse, and your family.
- Develop good coping tools and strategies.
- Find new ways of healing your own damaged self-esteem.
- Talk regularly with safe, supportive people and work hard to not isolate yourself from others.
- Practice forgiving yourself and your spouse.
- Experiment with different ways to defuse your own stresses and those between you and your spouse.
- Get into a daily habit of sharing the highs and lows of your day (the best things and worst things that have happened) and how you *feel* about them.
- Admit to yourself and God that you need his help controlling your mental health struggles.
- Turn your life and marriage over to the care and direction of God.

IF YOUR SPOUSE HAS A MENTAL ILLNESS:

- Develop realistic expectations for you, your spouse, and your marriage.
- Identify unhealthy patterns of communicating and relating in your marriage.
- Pinpoint the specific behaviors your mentally ill spouse exhibits that may be harming you and your children.
- Discover what emotions your spouse's mental

illness behavior has triggered in you and your children.

- Make necessary adjustments to ensure happiness and safety for you and your children.
- Seek advice about what to do if your spouse is suicidal, and make an action plan.
- Remind yourself, often, that your marriage is a lifelong commitment.
- Learn ways of dealing with your spouse's personality changes and your own damaged responses.
- Work at forgiving yourself and your spouse.
- Learn all you can about your spouse's illness and its treatments.
- Experiment with new ways of taking better care of yourself—physically, mentally, emotionally, and spiritually.
- Mentally condition yourself to fight your tendencies to withdraw from others who don't understand your situation or who might pile on guilt that you're not being a good enough spouse.
- Make it a habit to describe two positive qualities you've observed in your spouse in the past week, then share with him or her why those are important to you.
- Admit to yourself and God that your marriage stresses are out of control and that you can't handle them alone—you need his help.
- Turn your life and marriage over to the care and direction of God.

- Ask God for help in restoring positive feelings toward your spouse.
- Keep the focus on prayer. You might ask your spouse to pray for a specific situation you may face tomorrow, or you could describe an answer to prayer you've had in the past week.

If you and your spouse are able to discuss how your past is affecting your present, and if you make an effort to implement some of these ideas to help the marriage rebuilding process, you'll be well on your way to a healed relationship!

7

WHAT IF A SPOUSE IS UNWILLING TO GET HELP?

Though no one can go back and make a new start, anyone can start from new and make a brand new end.
Author Unknown

Healing and rebuilding your marriage may seem like an impossible task. Your energy and optimism are probably depleted, if not demolished. Your emotions may be frayed to the breaking point. But if possible, do *everything* you can to save your marriage.

However, if you've worked at your relationship for a long time and tried everything mentioned in this book but nothing is working, you may have to consider other hard options like separation or divorce.

Tragically, sometimes bipolar spouses remain in denial of their illness, or refuse to get help. This hard-lined attitude leads to ignorance of the devastating effects the disorder has on their family and causes endless, unbearable pain for their spouses. There is only so much physical, emotional, and financial stress a marriage or family can take. Healthy spouses eventually must make some hard choices for their own well-being and for their children's welfare.

The Bible teaches that married persons have a responsibility for meeting not only the material needs of their spouse and family, but also for their *emotional and spiritual* needs:

> *If anyone does not provide for his relatives, and especially for his immediate family, he has denied the faith and is worse than an unbeliever.* [3]

If you've exhausted your efforts through counseling and other means of repairing your marriage, and if your bipolar spouse still remains unresponsive, you may have to make a tough decision: keep trying to restore the marriage, or file for a legal separation or divorce.

If you reach this point, it is important to find a good attorney to help you understand the legal and financial realities you will face.

While there are differing interpretations of Scripture regarding divorce, we both believe that, for certain cases, there are biblical grounds for divorce. While it is a heartbreaking outcome, we support those who have been forced to make such painful choices. One helpful book that gives a good biblical perspective is *Divorce and Remarriage in the Church* by David Instone-Brewer.

If Jim had allowed his illness to take over, and if he had not been willing to take his medications, see his doctors, and be proactive in fighting against his bipolar symptoms, I'm not sure I could have hung in there. A spouse and a family can't continue to take the constant emotional and verbal abuse or live with someone who's unwilling to work at recovering from his or her illness.

However, I'm very, very blessed and enormously fortunate that Jim was willing to change and aggressively seek wellness. His efforts to heal and recover, and his willingness to be patient with me as I worked through my own issues, is what made our marriage work. I pray that you will experience this blessing too!

CONCLUSION

While we realize that we've barely scratched the surface of how we're working out our evolving, deepening relationship, we've shared these tips and strategies with the hope that some of them may be of help for you and your spouse.

Each marriage, of course, has its own needs. Therefore, your process of healing and rebuilding will be different than ours. You'll need to experiment and find what works best for you.

If you are ready to give up on your marriage, please keep in mind the old saying, "A perfect marriage is just two imperfect people who refuse to give up on each other!"

Our prayer is that God will guide, protect, and encourage you as you continue working at healing and rebuilding your marriage.

CAN YOU HELP ME WITH SOMETHING?

Thank you for reading this book and I hope you've been encouraged by it! If you've found it especially helpful and worthy of a recommendation, can you help me with something?

Will you please email me with a couple of sentences as a mini book review? You could share what you liked about the book and how it impacted your life. Potential readers will be encouraged by your words!

A portion of the profits from these books will be used to support four ministries: wounded veterans, mentally ill patients and families, career guidance, and clergy counseling.

WANT TO STAY UP-TO-DATE WITH MY NEW BOOKS AND ARTICLES?

Subscribe to my newsletter for great articles, behind-the-scenes looks at upcoming books, and a FREE digital copy of my book *9 Critical Steps to take in a Mental Health Crisis*.

Visit www.drjimstout.com/join to subscribe.

APPENDIX

Strategies in Review

We described a lot of strategies we used to heal our marriage, so we've listed them here for your convenience. When you don't have the time or energy to reread this whole book, please feel free to use this section as a quick reference.

HOW HAVE YOU INDIVIDUALLY COPED WITH THE EFFECTS OF BIPOLAR DISORDER?

Jim's Response:

- I studied literature on recovery and spiritual development.
- I searched for supportive people and sought out relationships and friendships.
- I attended support groups.
- I took personal responsibility for my actions.
- I learned to identify my triggers for relapses.

- I picked up ways to protect myself from unnecessarily harsh criticisms.
- I learned how and when to detach.
- I learned the therapeutic value of writing.
- I used the Serenity Prayer to cope.
- I learned to forgive myself & Leah.

Leah's Response:

- I learned to forgive myself and Jim.
- I saw our marriage as a lifelong commitment.
- I separated Jim from his illness.
- I found safe, supportive friends.
- I learned how to emotionally detach from Jim.
- I resigned as Jim's caregiver.
- I learned how to set boundaries.
- I learned the importance of timing.
- I found a new career role for my life.
- I made it a priority to keep my own emotional gas tank full.

WHAT HAVE YOU DONE TO HEAL YOUR MARRIAGE?

Jim's Response:

- I initiated daily communication about our feelings.
- I made time for weekly dates.
- I injected surprises and humor into our relationship.
- I took Leah on mini honeymoons.
- I found tools to manage my stress.

- I monitored my workload.
- I was careful to get enough sleep.
- I helped with household chores.
- I encouraged and affirmed Leah.
- I learned as much as I could about rebuilding our marriage.

Leah's Response:

- I went to professional counseling.
- I prayed, both for Jim and with him.
- I chose to reattach to Jim.
- I asked God for help to restore me from my hurt and mistrust.
- I took up hobbies we both enjoy.
- I alerted our sons to watch for warning signs of mania or depression.
- I worked on my sense of humor.
- I developed realistic expectations.

ACKNOWLEDGMENTS

We sincerely appreciate the following people for their help in making this book happen:

- Our editors, who gave valuable shaping and guidance in manuscript details: Andrew Kroeger and Stephanie Starr
- Our copy editors and proofreaders, who corrected grammar and typographic flaws: Shelley Atwood and Elijah Dove
- Our office helper, who copied, collated, stapled, and filed articles used in the research and production of this book: Stephen Reese
- Our computer technicians, who installed programs and fixed computer glitches: Taylor Allee and Mike Adler

RESOURCES

Carter, Jay, Psy. D. *Nasty Men: How to Stop Being Hurt by Them Without Stooping to Their Level.* New York: McGraw-Hill Books, 1993.

Carter, Jay, Psy. D. *Nasty Women: How to Stop Being Hurt by Them Without Stooping to Their Level.* New York: McGraw-Hill Books, 2003.

Dobson, James C., Dr. *Straight Talk to Men and Their Wives.* Nashville: W Publishing Group, 1980.

Forward, Susan, Ph.D., and Donna Frazier. *When Your Lover Is a Liar: Healing the Wounds of Deception and Betrayal.* New York: Harper Perennial, 1999.

Gottman, John, Ph.D. *The Seven Principles for Making Marriage Work.* New York: Three Rivers Press, 1999.

Gottman, John, Ph.D., Joan DeClaire, and Daniel Coleman. *The Relationship Cure: A 5 Step Guide to Strengthening Your Marriage, Family and Friendships.* New York: Three Rivers Press, 2001.

Gottman, John, Ph.D., Julie Schwartz, Ph.D., and Joan

DeClaire. *10 Lessons to Transform Your Marriage: America's Love Lab Experts Share Their Strategies for Strengthening Your Relationship.* New York: Three Rivers Press, 2006.

Gottman, John, Ph.D., and Nan Silver. *Why Marriages Succeed or Fail: And How You Can Make Yours Last.* New York: Simon & Schuster, 1994.

Hawkins, David. *Does Your Man Have the Blues? Understanding Male Depression and How It Affects You.* Eugene: Harvest House Publishers, 2004.

Instone-Brewer, David. *Divorce and Remarriage in the Church.* Downers Grove: Inter-Varsity Press, 2003.

Johnson, Sue, Dr. *Hold Me Tight: Seven Conversations for a Lifetime of Love.* New York: Little, Brown and Company, 2008.

Penner, Clifford L., and Joyce J. Penner. T*he Gift of Sex: A Guide to Sexual Fulfillment.* Nashville: W Publishing Group, 2003.

Penner, Clifford L., and Joyce J. Penner. *Restoring the Pleasure: Complete Step-by-Step Programs to Help Couples Overcome the Most Common Sexual Barriers.* Nashville: W Publishing Group, 1993.

Petersen, J. Allan. *The Myth of Greener Grass: Affair-Proof Your Marriage, Restore Your Love, Recover Your Dreams.* Carol Stream: Tyndale House, 1984.

Schlessinger, Laura, Dr. *10 Stupid Things Couples Do to Mess Up Their Relationships.* New York: HarperCollins, 2002.

Schlessinger, Laura, Dr. *The Proper Care and Feeding of Marriage.* New York: HarperCollins, 2007.

Wright, H. Norman. *The Other Woman in Your Marriage: Understanding a Mother's Impact on Her Son and*

How It Affects His Marriage. Ventura: Gospel Light Publications, 1995.

Yerkovich, Milan, and Kay Yerkovich. *How We Love: A Revolutionary Approach to Deeper Connections in Marriage.* Colorado Springs: WaterBrook Press, 2006.

NOTES

1. "Managing Bipolar Disorder," *Psychology Today*, November 2003.
2. Ibid.
3. 1 Timothy 5:8 NIV

OTHER BOOKS BY DR. JIM STOUT

Dr. Stout has been a pastor, leader, husband, and loving father, yet in the past he's also been clinically depressed and suicidal. His easy-to-read books describe his experiences and recovery. They share the techniques he used to heal himself and offer you tools to reclaim your life and move forward!

All books are (or soon will be) available online through Amazon. Further information can be found by visiting Dr. Stout's website at www.drjimstout.com.

Please consider purchasing some of these life-enhancing publications for yourself, or as gifts for family members, friends, patients, clergy, and mental and medical health providers. They are ideal for encouragement gifts, bulk orders, special promotions, and other uses.

A portion of the profits will be used for various mental illness, wounded veterans, clergy, and career-guidance ministries.

rebuilding
your life

bipolar disorder

A BIPOLAR'S STORY

THAT INCLUDES PRACTICAL

STRATEGIES, TECHNIQUES

AND TIPS FOR MANAGING MOODS

Rev. Dr. James T. Stout

BIPOLAR DISORDER—REBUILDING YOUR LIFE

A Bipolar's Story That Includes Practical Strategies, Techniques, and Tips for Managing Moods

This is the true story of one man's battle to recover from depression, mania, the stigma of mental illness, and the trauma of childhood emotional and sexual abuse.

Visit www.drjimstout.com/books for more information.

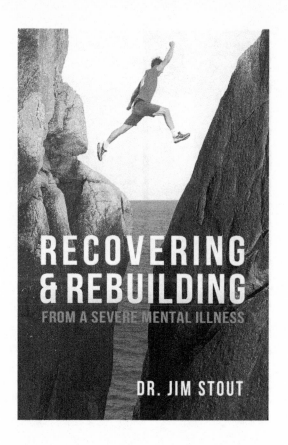

RECOVERING AND REBUILDING FROM A SEVERE MENTAL ILLNESS

This short, gripping book candidly shares Dr. Stout's story of faith and his battles with clinical depression, suicidal thinking, bipolar disorder, sexual abuse, and post-traumatic stress disorder (PTSD). Includes many helpful suggestions for other strugglers.

Visit <u>www.drjimstout.com/books</u> for more information.

BOUNDARY SETTING FOR CLERGY AND MINISTRY WORKERS

Tired of never having enough time or never pleasing your congregation? Help is here! This book is built on lessons from the trenches of 45 years in pastoral and parachurch ministries. Jam-packed with practical tools. A must read for those in ministries and helping professions.

Visit   www.drjimstout.com/books   for   more information.

BOUNDARY SETTING

A Practical Guide

"How can I better handle pressure from others? What can I do to keep my schedule under control?" This book is filled with practical how-tos based on lessons from the trenches of 45 years of counseling and leadership. A must read for those who need help setting or maintaining boundaries!

Visit www.drjimstout.com/books for more information.

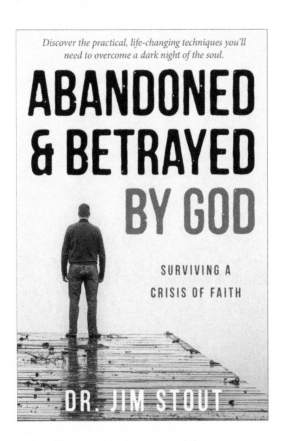

Discover the practical, life-changing techniques you'll need to overcome a dark night of the soul.

ABANDONED & BETRAYED BY GOD

BY GOD

SURVIVING A CRISIS OF FAITH

DR. JIM STOUT

ABANDONED AND BETRAYED BY GOD

Surviving a Crisis of Faith

This is a brutally honest account of a Christian leader's struggle with his faith. It reveals how he coped with distressing obstacles and the roads he took to eventually deepen his connection with God. Includes biblical guidelines and numerous practical tips.

Visit   www.drjimstout.com/books   for   more information.

9 CRITICAL STEPS TO TAKE IN A MENTAL HEALTH CRISIS

Perfect for those needing help coping and overcoming unmet or shattered expectations, this book is packed with useful suggestions to help you recover from your broken dreams.

Visit www.drjimstout.com/books for more information.

24 battle-proven suggestions to help you recover from your broken dreams

CRUSHED HOPES

Overcoming Unmet Expectations

DR. JIM STOUT

CRUSHED HOPES

Overcoming Unmet Expectations

If you need help in coping with and overcoming unmet expectations, this book is for you. It will help you let go of unmet expectations, develop realistic expectations, draw on spiritual sources for strength, navigate your relationships carefully, and maintain the right mindset.

Visit www.drjimstout.com/books for more information.

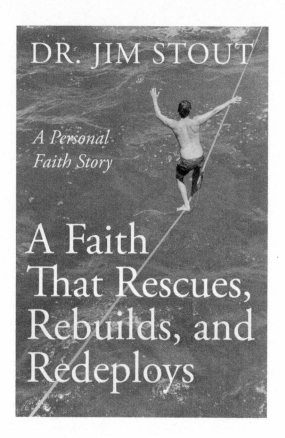

A FAITH THAT RESCUES, REBUILDS, AND REDEPLOYS

This short book shares the story of Dr. Stout's seemingly catastrophic childhood and how he was finally able to use a newfound faith in Christ to turn these early setbacks into a life of helping others. Dr. Stout also shows how you too can accept Christ to find purpose and transformation in your life.

Visit <u>www.drjimstout.com/books</u> for more information.

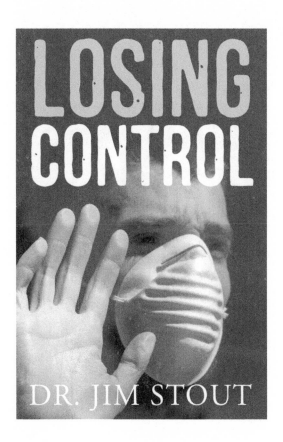

LOSING CONTROL

How to Cope When Everything Around You Is Changing

When an unexpected crisis hits, worry escalates. Some fight, some flee. Others numb themselves with addictive substances or behaviors. This book offers battle-tested suggestions for coping with or overcoming helpless feelings of being out-of-control.

Visit   www.drjimstout.com/books   for   more information.

INSIDE THE MIND OF A SUICIDAL CHRISTIAN
LEADER AND HOW HE SURVIVED

WRITINGS OF PAIN, WRITINGS OF HOPE

DR. JIM STOUT

WRITINGS OF PAIN, WRITINGS OF HOPE

Candid Thoughts of a Suicidally Depressed Christian Leader and How He Survived

A collection of writings and journaling that will inject you with hopefulness, this book gives a candid glimpse into the thinking of a depressed and suicidal Christian leader.

Visit   www.drjimstout.com/books   for   more information.

Practical tips and techniques to get you through any stressful situation.

STRESS BUSTING

HOW TO REDUCE ANXIETY & TENSION IN YOUR LIFE

DR. JIM STOUT

STRESS BUSTING

This book is for those feeling weighed down, overwhelmed, stressed, anxious, or resentful due to relationship tensions, situation-induced strains, or self-made pressures. Filled with helpful suggestions for avoiding or handling unnecessary anxieties. Coming soon!

Visit www.drjimstout.com/books for more information.

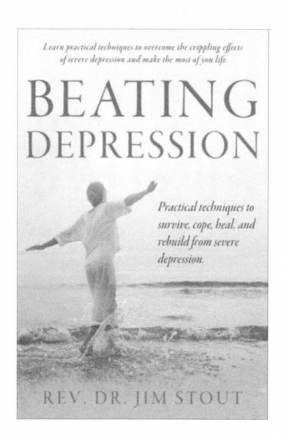

BEATING DEPRESSION

A hands-on manual for reclaiming your life from the claws of depression. This book is for those who suffer with depression and for their loved ones who want to help but don't know how. Packed with practical strategies and ways to survive, cope, heal, and rebuild from unyielding depression. Coming soon!

Visit www.drjimstout.com/books for more information.

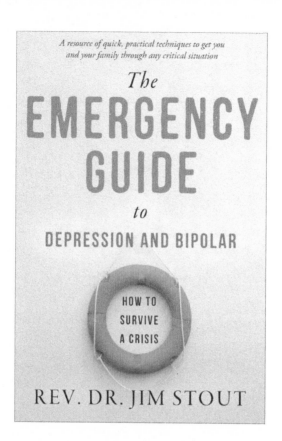

A resource of quick, practical techniques to get you and your family through any critical situation

The

EMERGENCY GUIDE

to

DEPRESSION AND BIPOLAR

HOW TO
SURVIVE
A CRISIS

REV. DR. JIM STOUT

THE EMERGENCY GUIDE TO DEPRESSION AND BIPOLAR DISORDER

How to Survive a Crisis

This guidebook offers suggestions for those battling a severe depressive or manic episode or suicidal thinking. It also gives specific what-to-do information for their loved ones who want to be supportive and helpful but don't know how. Coming soon!

Visit   www.drjimstout.com/books   for   more information.

BUILDING A STRONGER MARRIAGE AND FAMILY

Based on the personal experiences of Jim and Leah Stout, who've been married over fifty years, this book offers down-to-earth strategies for strengthening your marriage and parenting skills. Dr. Stout has counseled hundreds of newlyweds, new parents, parents of teenagers, and parents of adult children. Coming soon!

Visit www.drjimstout.com/books for more information.

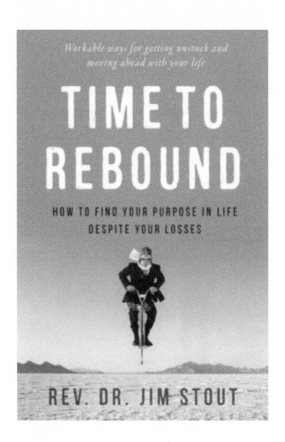

TIME TO REBOUND

How to Find Your Purpose in Life despite Your Losses

Countless people keep busy on an endless cycle of self-pity, frustration, and boredom, hoping to rediscover their life purpose. Don't let that be you! Learn workable ways for getting unstuck and moving ahead with your life. Coming soon!

Visit www.drjimstout.com/books for more information.

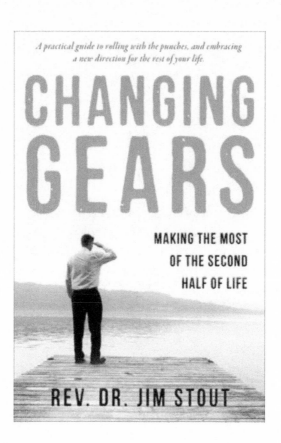

A practical guide to rolling with the punches, and embracing a new direction for the rest of your life.

CHANGING GEARS

MAKING THE MOST OF THE SECOND HALF OF LIFE

REV. DR. JIM STOUT

CHANGING GEARS

Making the Most of the Second Half of Life

For those whose job or career has soured or ended and are wanting to start over and make the most of the second half of life. This book provides motivation, support, and concrete steps for re-inventing yourself and getting the most from your coming years. Coming soon!

Visit <u>www.drjimstout.com/books</u> for more information.

ABOUT THE AUTHORS

LEAH STOUT

Rev. Leah A. Stout was raised in Cleveland Heights, Ohio. She graduated from Miami University in 1967 with a bachelor's degree in education and married Jim Stout that same year.

They have two grown children: Jim Stout, Jr., who works for an insurance company, and John, who is a teacher with special-needs and autistic children. Jim and Leah also have four marvelous grandchildren.

Leah taught elementary school while Jim finished his Master of Divinity degree at Gordon-Conwell Theological Seminary in Massachusetts.

In 1991, Leah began a ten-year commitment to earning her Master of Divinity degree at Fuller Theological Seminary in Pasadena, California. In 1993, she was hired part-time at St. Andrew's Presbyterian Church to do hospital visitations.

She graduated from Fuller in 2001 and became the full-time Minister of Congregational Care at St. Andrew's in 2002, and was ordained in March of 2003. In July of 2015, she "retired" from full-time work, and now continues her ministry on the staff at St. Andrew's a few days a week.

Leah enjoys travel, reading, walking, and music. But, her primary interest, now that she has more free time, is getting "Grandma Fixes"—times with her four energetic grandchildren.

DR. JIM STOUT

Dr. Jim Stout is an ordained Presbyterian minister who has pastored in five churches. His other ministry experiences include working with college and graduate students at Harvard, MIT, Boston, Northeastern, and Miami universities; doing social work with Young Life's outreach to teenage gangs in New York City; and working as student chaplain to the men's violent ward at Danvers Massachusetts State Mental Hospital.

He was given the National Alliance for the Mentally Ill (NAMI) California's "Distinguished Clergy Award" for his efforts on behalf of those affected by mental illness.

In college, he participated in varsity football and wrestling, and won Golden Gloves heavyweight boxing championships in Pennsylvania and Ohio. Since then, he has competed in triathlons, and at almost age 70, he finished seven- and eight-day *Ride2Recovery* group rides on his recumbent bike to raise money for wounded war veterans.

He received his Master of Divinity from Gordon-

Conwell Theological Seminary and his Doctor of Ministry from Fuller Theological Seminary.

He has been married to the former Leah Ann Hayden since 1967. They have two sons, Jim Jr. and John, and six energetic grandchildren.

Find out more at his website: www.drjimstout.com

Made in the USA
Monee, IL
11 May 2021

68329584R00069